COLLECTIVE WORSHIP FOR SECONDARY SCHOOLS

Ready-to-use assemblies

Mike Anderson and Martin Grace

Kevin Mayhew

First published in 2001 by
KEVIN MAYHEW LTD
Buxhall, Stowmarket
Suffolk IP14 3BW
Email: info@kevinmayhewltd.com

9 8 7 6 5 4 3 2 1 0

ISBN 1 84003 807 1
Catalogue No 1500457

Illustrations by Steve English
Cover design by Jonathan Stroulger
Edited by Elisabeth Bates
Typeset by Louise Selfe

Printed in Great Britain

Contents

This resource pack is dedicated to all the pupils
who have let us walk with them on their faith journeys –
during the daily act of Collective Worship.

Acknowledgements

The publishers wish to express their gratitude to the following for permission
to include copyright material in this book:

Stainer & Bell Ltd, PO Box 110, Victoria House, 23 Gruneisen Road, London
N3 1DZ, for the extract from *Lord of the Dance* by Sydney Carter, © 1963,
Stainer & Bell Ltd.

Hodder & Stoughton Publishers, 338 Euston Road, London, NW1 3BH, for
the prayer 'Goodness is stronger than evil' by Desmond Tutu.

Every effort has been made to trace the owners of copyright material and we
hope that no copyright has been infringed. Pardon is sought and apology
made if the contrary be the case, and a correction will be made in any
reprint of this book.

Overview

By law, schools are legally obliged to provide a daily act of collective worship. Logistically this can be a big problem for teachers. Many non-specialists are given the task of leading prayers with their form during registration time – the available time stretching from just a couple of minutes to a sometimes quite uncomfortable 10 minutes. Understandably, there can be a lack of confidence to try things out which, coupled with other demands which leave little time for preparation of materials, can mean that prayer time is not the sort of experience that enriches either pupils or teachers.

Included is a host of resource materials for those charged with the awesome responsibility of leading young people in prayer on a daily basis.

- The materials have been tried and tested through the full age range of an 11-16 secondary school, but some resources would certainly be usable with older children in junior schools.

- The materials are based around themes such as 'Hollywood Films', 'Plays of Shakespeare' or 'The Gifts of the Spirit'.

- Within each theme (lasting from three to seven weeks) are materials for each week.

- The materials vary from theme to theme but include two minute introductions, short reflections, mini-biographies, scripture passages and reflections, and pupil activities of varying length – all of which can be adapted to individual circumstances.

- Each week has a photocopiable 'prayer of the week' for wall display.

- Materials can also be used as a resource for assembly providers.

- With each theme come suggestions for display and relevant music.

A time for . . .

A seven-week series based on Ecclesiastes 3

A time for . . . PLANTING

INTRODUCTION

In Western society, the idea of planting a seed, tending it and eventually harvesting a crop has lost much of its meaning because we get so much food that is pre-packaged. People in other continents like Asia and Africa have a much better understanding of planting. They need to know which seeds to plant where, when to plant, how deep to plant, how far apart seeds should be planted and so on. Their lives depend on getting these things right. If they get them right and the weather is kind, then their seeds will develop and they will have what they need to live.

To a certain extent, our own lives depend on how we choose to develop our attitudes. Take the opportunity this week to think about the attitudes you would like to plant and develop – attitudes towards others, towards work, towards play and towards God.

ACTIVITY

Ask your pupils about the seeds they would like to sow in the world – they could be seeds which bring happiness, laughter, less suffering in the world, etc. Ask them to think about the seeds that they would like to plant in their own lives – maybe being more organised, hardworking, less easily offended, less likely to hurt others, more willing to put others first, and so on.

Ask pupils to write these down. It would be in keeping with the theme if they could write them down on small circles ('seeds'). Then collect them in and display them or keep them safe until later in the year when they can be looked at again to see if any of the 'seeds' have developed.

GOSPEL STORY (Mark 4:30-32)

Jesus said: **'The kingdom of heaven is like a mustard seed. Even though this is the smallest of all seeds, when it grows it is the biggest shrub of all and has such large branches that the birds come and take shelter in them.'**

In the English language we have many similes – as thin as a rake, as brave as a lion, as quiet as a mouse, for example. Can you think of any more? At the time of Jesus, there was a Jewish simile: 'as small as a mustard seed'. Jesus uses this to encourage his few followers not to be discouraged, because eventually their number would grow. At the end of the second millennium an estimated 33.2 per cent of the world's population were followers of Jesus. Jesus makes a difference to their lives. His Gospel values of love and justice and serving others make a difference in the world. Let's pray that these values will make a difference to us. Then we can make a difference in school, at home, in our communities and in the world.

SPECIAL PERSON

Rosa Parks was an ordinary black woman in 1960s America. One day, after she had finished work and then shopping for her family, she got on the bus home. She sat down, tired. The bus started to fill up and a white man went to Rosa, expecting her to stand up for him. (At the time, blacks were supposed to stand up so that whites could sit.) She stayed sitting and was arrested.

When the other members of the black community heard this, they decided they had to act. For a whole year, no black got on a bus until the bus company had lost so much money that they got rid of the rule that said whites were better than blacks. Imagine it, for a whole year, blacks walked long distances, to work, to the shops. They left home early in the morning and returned late at night. But they never gave up. Rosa Parks had planted a seed of non-violent resistance in them and this inspired their crusade for justice. A little-known minister was particularly inspired and he took up the leadership of their cause. You may not have heard of Rosa Parks, but you will probably know the name of this minister – Martin Luther King.

PRAYER

Lord, sometimes I feel bad about myself –
my self-esteem is as small as a mustard seed.
Sometimes, my love for others
is as small as a mustard seed.
Sometimes, my belief in you
is as small as a mustard seed.

Lord, help me to grow in self-esteem,
in love for others and in faith in you. Amen.

A time for . . . HEALING

INTRODUCTION

Our bodies are amazing things. If we cut ourselves, or catch a cold, the body basically heals itself. We do have to go to the doctors sometimes; these days they can perform some fantastic procedures which were unthinkable only a few decades ago – things like transplants and micro-surgery.

There has also been a tremendous growth over the last few years in 'complementary medicine' – things like aromatherapy, herbalism and acupuncture.

However, doctors cannot help us heal the hurts we cause each other in our relationships. We can cause hurt by name-calling, by what we do and say, and by whom we exclude. This week, we are going to think about the healing of the spirit. We cannot very often heal our own hurts. We need others to help us do that. However, we can help heal the hurts we have caused others. This week, let's think about how we can heal others – how we can be spirit doctors – and ask God for the sensitivity and courage to be active healers.

ACTIVITY

If you have ever been in a dentist's waiting room, you will have experienced the 'delights' of *Readers' Digest*. One of the regular features is 'Laughter Is the Best Medicine'. Laughter is very good physiologically as well as psychologically. Why not, as part of your prayer time this week, have a laughter slot and give pupils a chance to share jokes? (A couple of minutes at afternoon registration might be a good time.) Why not run a 'caption competition' by taking in a photo and asking pupils to come up with a funny caption? The emphasis is on 'having a laugh' together. It's also a chance to talk with pupils about the difference between 'laughing with' and 'laughing at'.

You could close each session with the simple prayer:
Lord, thank you for laughter. Amen.

GOSPEL STORY (Mark 1:40-42)

A leper came to Jesus, knelt before him and said: 'If you want to – you can heal me.' Jesus felt sorry for the man and reached out and touched him saying, 'Of course I want to! Be healed!' And the leprosy left him at once and he was cured.

Leprosy is a terrible disease. A couple of years ago, Blue Peter ran an appeal to help sufferers who often lose the use of parts of their body as a result of leprosy. It is also a disease which disfigures. At the time of Jesus, lepers were treated as outcasts. They were not allowed to live in the villages and towns and had to stay away from people and ring bells and shout, 'unclean! unclean!' if they came near anyone, to warn them. They were de-humanised. The most significant part of this story is not that Jesus had the power to heal – but that Jesus reached out and touched him – treating him like a fellow human being.

In our society, we very often treat the mentally handicapped or the disabled badly. We might shy away from them or stare at them or use hurtful terms like 'spaz'. We might treat classmates as outcasts by talking about them behind their backs or excluding them from our groups. This week, make a special effort to reach out to others and not treat them as outcasts.

SPECIAL PERSON

Leonard Cheshire was born in 1917 in Cheshire. During World War II, he was a pilot in the famous Dam Busters Squadron and he won the Victoria Cross for bravery. In 1945, he was one of the British observers who witnessed the dropping of the atomic bomb on Nagasaki. The bomb killed 40,000 people.

After the war, Leonard tried a number of jobs. He tried to set up a home for ex-servicemen but it failed. His life was changed when a colleague, Arthur Dykes, who was dying from cancer, had no one to look after him. Leonard took him into his own home and was amazed at how Arthur's belief in God helped him through his pain and subsequent death. Eventually, Leonard himself became a Christian and his new-found faith inspired him to open his home to others who were sick but had no one to look after them. This was the first Cheshire Home.

Leonard devoted his life to help those who were suffering and though he never gained any medical qualifications, he helped in the healing of many people's loneliness and helplessness. Leonard died in 1992, by which time there were 85 Cheshire Homes in the UK and 185 in 50 countries overseas.

PRAYER

Love beyond measure, mercy so free,
your endless resources, given to me,
strength to the weary, healing our lives,
your love beyond measure has opened my eyes. Amen.

A time for . . . BUILDING

INTRODUCTION

One of the first toys we get as children is a set of building bricks. Have you noticed, though, how much easier it is for a baby to knock over a tower that has been built than to actually build the tower? As the child grows older though, he or she gets more pleasure out of building houses or walls. The child moves on to Duplo or Lego and these bricks help them create their own world in which they can play for hours.

This week we are going to think about building and the choices we face in our relationships. Basically, we can be builders of **steps**, **walls** or **bridges**.

Builders of **steps** like to make themselves look more important than others. They like to get on their steps and look down on others.

Builders of **walls** like to keep some people or things close to them and to keep other people and things away from them. Builders of **walls** can be selfish in their relationships. While they might not think of themselves as superior to others, they do not feel they have much to learn from others – preferring to be left alone with what they are comfortable with within their walls.

Builders of **bridges** like to experience new ideas and want to reach out to others. Bridges are more difficult to build than either steps or walls, so builders of **bridges** need to be quite determined and resilient.

Christians are called to build the kingdom of God here and now. It is a kingdom of **bridges**. This week consider what you build.

ACTIVITY

The song for Comic Relief 1995 contained the following words:

'Love can build a bridge – between your heart and mine.
Love can build a bridge – don't you think it's time?
Don't you think it's time?'

Do a class brainstorm on people and issues which need a bridge to unite them (most effective if you have a bridge already drawn on a large piece of sugar paper).

Examples: Catholics and Protestants in Northern Ireland, the poor and the rich, those with jobs and those without jobs, parents and teenagers.

Finish with a simple prayer like:

Help us, Lord, to build bridges rather than steps and walls. Amen.

SPECIAL PERSON

About 10 years ago, an ordinary man became a hero because he built a very special bridge.

The *Herald of Free Enterprise* was a huge passenger ferry which crossed the Channel daily. One day, it left Zeebrugge and one of the crew failed to secure the bow doors. As a result, water flooded into the lower car-deck of the ship and it started to sink. Over 170 people died in this disaster, but it would have been more had it not been for this man who formed himself into a human bridge to allow other passengers to clamber to safety over him.

Fortunately we are not likely to be in such a position, but we can make the effort to build bridges to help other people around us.

PRAYER

Lord God, your creation shows me
how wonderful the world can be.
Jesus, your example shows me
how to make the world a better place.
Holy Spirit, give me the courage
to build the kingdom of God – here and now. Amen.

A time for . . . SILENCE

INTRODUCTION

Silence can be very special. After the Hillsborough disaster in 1989, thousands of people made a pilgrimage to Anfield to lay their scarves or flowers there in remembrance of those who had died. As they filed through the ground, they were silent. It was a special moment for anyone who experienced it.

On Armistice Day, two minutes silence is now kept again throughout the country in memory of those who died in two World Wars. Radio stations, supermarket tills and school classrooms fall silent.

In these cases, silence is a sign of respect, but silence can also be very awkward. It can be really embarrassing when you are with someone and realise you have nothing to say to them. It gets even worse when you try to think of something – only to find your mind has gone blank.

This week we are going to think about the right time to be silent. Sometimes things are better left unsaid. We often regret things we say in anger, on the spur of the moment – remember when Kevin Keegan lost his rag in an outburst against Alec Ferguson. And yet, sometimes we stay silent when we should speak up – we maintain a 'conspiracy of silence'.

We are going to ask God this week to help us in our decisions as to when to be silent and when not to be.

ACTIVITY

Hand out pieces of paper and ask pupils to reflect on 'Things I Wish I'd Never Said'. Times when they may have said things they regret might include:

- saying something hurtful to someone else;
- boasting about something or other;
- making an unkeepable promise.

When they have written them down, pupils could be asked to share what they've written. Then pupils could be given the opportunity to reflect in the following way:

So, let's think about why we regret saying these things. (pause)
Let's think about who ended up hurt. (pause)
Let's pray for that person, asking God to heal any hurt. (pause)
Let's think about any way in which we could put things right. (pause)
Let's ask God to help us put things right. (pause)

And now, let's get rid of these things we've said –
let's rip them up and throw them away –
and leave them behind us.

GOSPEL STORY (Matthew 6:1-4)

And Jesus said to them:

'Be careful not to parade your good deeds before others to attract their attention. If you do this, you will lose all reward from your Father in heaven. When you give money to help others, do not tell everyone about it. This is what the hypocrites do to win people's admiration. They have already received their reward. No, when you help someone, do not let your left hand know what your right hand is doing, and your Father in heaven – who sees all that is done in secret – will reward you.'

This is quite difficult to come to terms with. Most people want to help others, but it is also nice if other people notice and praise us for it. Why not do something for others this week and keep it to yourself?

SPECIAL PERSON

During World War II, a British girl called Odette Churchill was parachuted into France to help the Resistance Movement organise the escape of shot-down pilots.

Odette was captured by the Gestapo and suffered terrible torture, but she did not betray any member of the Resistance Movement. Even the brutal expertise of the Gestapo could not break her spirit. Odette survived the war and her story was made into a film.

It's a salutary lesson for us who are often only too willing to 'drop others in it'. Maybe today's challenge could be to hold our tongues, rather than use them at other people's expense.

PRAYER

God, give me the patience to hold my tongue
when I should be silent.
Give me the courage to speak out
when I should speak out.
But most of all, give me the wisdom
to know the difference. Amen.

A time for . . . CELEBRATING

INTRODUCTION

No doubt we can all remember the way we celebrated the dawn of the new millennium: parties, fireworks, cards and so on. There is no doubt that times have changed over the last hundred years, never mind the last two thousand years. For example:

The last century saw the invention of the aeroplane, television, personal computers, Walkman – the list goes on and on! All of these would have seemed miraculous to the people of the nineteenth century. What 'miraculous' innovations will this century bring?

What has not changed though, is the Christian's mission to be a living example of the message of Jesus, to build the kingdom of God according to the gospel values of love and justice. No doubt there have been many times when we have failed, but this week let's celebrate those things we have achieved!

ACTIVITY

We often use the term 'celebrity' to indicate that a person is well known. You'll be able to name plenty of celebrities yourself. However, a celebrity is someone whose life and achievements should be celebrated. And so – we are all celebrities! Today, let's celebrate our own gifts. Let's think about what we have brought to our school. It may be a sense of humour; it may be the gift of making friends; it may be the gift of not badmouthing others.

Have a class brainstorm on what gifts they bring between them. Then display it in your class. You can close by thanking God for the gift of each other and challenging the pupils to celebrate each other – to say something positive about someone else as often as possible.

GOSPEL STORY (Luke 15:3-7)

The Pharisees and teachers of the Law were criticising Jesus for being friendly with sinners so Jesus told them this parable:

'Suppose one of you has a hundred sheep and loses one of them – what do you do? You leave the other ninety-nine sheep in the wilderness and go looking for the one that got lost until you find it. When you find it, you are so happy that you put it on your shoulders and carry it back home. Then you call your friends and neighbours together and say to them, "I am so happy I found my lost sheep. Let us celebrate!"'

At the time of Jesus, shepherds were not regarded very highly. In fact, they were often the butt of jokes in the same way that these days the Irish are often unjustifiably ridiculed. Jesus actually describes a pretty strange situation. Surely the last thing you would do if you lost one sheep from among a hundred would be to leave the ninety-nine in the desert to wander off or be attacked by wolves? But, if you look at the story as an example of how much God loves us – it's very profound. God's love for those who wander off is so strong. Maybe you have drifted away from God's love or shut God out of your life. Maybe you don't feel good enough to try to develop a relationship with God. Nonsense! – God loves you and will welcome you back anytime. You're special! Celebrate your specialness and give yourself a chance to pray this week.

SPECIAL PERSON

Some years ago, our nation celebrated the release of Terry Waite, who was an adviser to the Anglican Archbishop of Canterbury. In 1981, Terry had helped to negotiate the release of some British hostages from Iran. In 1985, he managed to get Libya to release some British hostages. Each time, he put himself in considerable danger in order to prove to the hostage-takers that he was a man of integrity. However, in January 1987, while trying to negotiate the release of some hostages in Lebanon, he was himself taken prisoner. Terry spent over three years in a room two metres square, in solitary confinement. The only thing that got him through was his belief that God was watching over him. He was eventually released in November 1991.

He is an example of the tremendous strength that can be gained when we place our problems before God. The answers do come, although not necessarily as quickly as we want, nor in the way we expect them.

PRAYER

Lord, help me to smile and laugh
whate'er my mortal state.
Yes, even in life's darkest hour,
Lord, help me to celebrate. Amen.

A time for . . . DANCING

INTRODUCTION

This week our theme is 'A time for . . . DANCING'.

Dancing is a world-wide phenomenon. All cultures have dances which are part of their heritage. Dancing, though, has its fashions – some members of staff will remember the jive, the bump, and the dance to the Birdie Song! (Although they probably won't demonstrate them unless you ask politely!) American line dancing is popular at the moment and *Riverdance* and *Lord of the Dance* are enjoying worldwide success; ballroom dancing may soon become an Olympic event.

Dancing, whether stylised or improvised, expresses a personal response to music and reveals something about the dancer. The prevailing emotions expressed through dance are joy and love. Dancing is one way in which you can express the 'inner self'.

This week, we will be thinking about our 'inner selves' and how we, as humans, need to express our feelings and beliefs – not necessarily through dance, but through religion. Give yourself a chance this week to look for the good things in God's creation – in yourself and in other people – and 'dance your own dance' in response.

ACTIVITY

There are many types of dance. Ask pupils to brainstorm as many different dances as they can in two minutes. Each dance expresses emotion in a different way; ask pupils to decide which dance most closely fits in with their own personality (e.g. graceful like ballet, energetic like the jive, wanting to fit in with everyone else – line dancing).

Ask which dance most closely fits members of their family, and finally ask which dance most closely fits their idea of God. (Can they imagine God dancing at all?) Pupils can discuss in pairs, groups or as a class. Close with a short prayer like:

Lord, thank you for the joy of dance. Amen.

OLD TESTAMENT READING (ZEPHANIAH 3:14-17)

Sing and shout for joy, people of Israel! Rejoice with all your heart, Jerusalem! The Lord has ended your punishment; he has removed all your enemies. The Lord, the king of Israel, is with you; there is no reason now to be afraid.

The time is coming when they will say to Jerusalem, 'Do not be afraid, city of Zion! Do not let your hands hang limp! The Lord your God is with you; his power gives you victory. The Lord will take delight in you, and in his love he will give you new life. He will dance with shouts of joy over you as on a day of festival.'

When we think of God the Father it tends to be as a sort of Santa Claus figure in white robes, sitting on a throne looking down on us. However, this reading gives a very different picture indeed. God loves us through all our difficulties, and when we triumph God DANCES over us and SHOUTS for us. This should encourage us and remind us that – whether we are aware of it or not – God is always there for us. We are special – so special that our God (the God of the universe) – takes delight in our seemingly insignificant lives and DANCES with joy for us.

SPECIAL PERSON

You may remember Roy Castle, the presenter of *Record Breakers*, who died of cancer a few years ago. He was an incredibly talented man – an accomplished musician and a brilliant tap-dancer.

What Roy Castle is remembered for, though, is the great fight he put up against cancer. He fought the disease for a number of years and confounded doctors with his resilience and cheerfulness. Before he died he said that he did not want people to be sad at his death, and at his own request a jazz band played at his memorial service.

Roy Castle has probably had more influence on people's lives because of the way he died than he ever did as a successful entertainer and presenter. His courage and zest for life in the most difficult situation make him a great role model.

PRAYER

Lord, you danced in the morning when the world was begun
and you danced in the moon and the stars and the sun.
You came down from heaven and you danced on the earth.
At Bethlehem you had your birth.
Lord, thank you! Amen.

A time for . . . LOOKING BACK

INTRODUCTION

One of the most popular tracks on the Oasis album *What's the Story (Morning Glory)* – one of the biggest selling records of the 1990s – is 'Don't Look Back in Anger'. Looking back – reviewing – reflecting – these are all perfectly natural human instincts. It's good to look back, but only if we do it in the right way.

Adults often look back through 'rose-coloured spectacles' and think everything was much better in the 'good old days'. And it's good to be sentimental about special times in our lives. Adults tend to be pretty selective about some of these memories though and, although they say the good old days were best, they are quite prepared to tell youngsters today how lucky they are. There's a famous sketch devised by the Monty Python team where some ageing self-made businessmen reflect on the terrible childhood they had, each trying to outdo the other in the awfulness of it all. It culminates in one claiming he lived in a shoebox in the middle of the motorway, ate gravel because the family was so poor, and had to get up three hours before he went to bed, so he could go to work for an employer whom he had to pay for the privilege of having his limbs chopped off!

Looking back is a good thing to do, especially if we learn something from it. There are often times in our lives when things go horribly wrong and we just don't understand why. But some time later, we can see that at least something can be salvaged from the wreckage – even if it is only that we had the strength to get through it somehow. Often it is in the darkest moments that we experience God. This week, as we look back, let's try to find something good in what has happened this term so far.

ACTIVITY

WOW!

Ask pupils to reflect on 'wow!' moments in their lives. 'Wow!' moments are those times when you're left in awe by something or someone. It can be an ambition realised, a 'first' experience of something, a song, a moment when you felt completely fulfilled, a moment when you felt God was close.

Close with the simple prayer:
Lord, thank you for my special memories.
Amen.

SPECIAL PERSON

Just imagine it – you have been imprisoned for 26 years because you have campaigned against injustices in your country. For 26 years you are denied freedom. For 26 years you have to sleep in a cell while the people who put you there live in luxury. For 26 years you dream of being free and ending the injustices your people suffer.

Then, you are set free. Within five years you become the most powerful person in your nation. You have the chance to punish those who imprisoned you. What would you do? Would you imprison them? Have them expelled from your country? Would you enjoy seeing them suffer?

This happened to a man recently – and instead of looking back in anger and seeking to get his revenge, he decided on a policy of reconciliation. Even though many of his people wanted revenge, he counselled them against it. There are problems still but his country is a place of hope now – not hatred. It is a nation that is working for the future. The nation is South Africa – the Rainbow Nation. The man's name – Nelson Rolihlahla Mandela.

PRAYER

Lord, when I look back I feel I have let myself down.
Lord, when I look back I see people I have hurt.
Lord, when I look back I hear cruel words I have said.

Lord, help me to move forward, confident that you forgive me.
Amen.

A TIME FOR PLANTING

Lord, sometimes I feel bad about myself –
my self-esteem is as small as a mustard seed.

Sometimes, my love for others
is as small as a mustard seed.

Sometimes, my belief in you
is as small as a mustard seed.

Lord, help me to grow in self-esteem,
in love for others and in faith in you.

Amen.

A TIME FOR HEALING

Love beyond measure, mercy so free,

your endless resources, given to me,

strength to the weary, healing our lives,

your love beyond measure has opened my eyes.

Amen.

A TIME FOR BUILDING

Lord God, your creation shows me
how wonderful the world can be.

Jesus, your example shows me
how to make the world a better place.

Holy Spirit, give me the courage
to build the kingdom of God – here and now.

Amen.

A TIME FOR SILENCE

God, give me the patience to hold my tongue
when I should be silent.

Give me the courage to speak out
when I should speak out.

But most of all, give me the wisdom
to know the difference.

Amen.

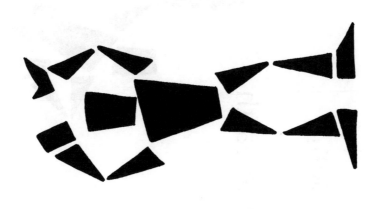

A TIME FOR CELEBRATING

Lord, help me to smile and laugh

whate'er my mortal state.

Yes, even in life's darkest hour,

Lord, help me celebrate.

Amen.

A TIME FOR DANCING

Lord, you danced in the morning when the world was begun

and you danced in the moon and the stars and the sun.

You came down from heaven and you danced on the earth.

At Bethlehem you had your birth.

Lord, thank you!

Amen.

A TIME FOR LOOKING BACK

Lord, when I look back I feel I have let myself down.

Lord, when I look back I see people I have hurt.

Lord, when I look back I hear cruel words I have said.

Lord, help me to move forward,

confident that you forgive me.

Amen.

Display Idea for 'A time for . . .' Theme

Set aside an area in the room and bring in appropriate artefacts/symbols each week to develop the area (suggestions below).

Week 1   **A time for . . . Planting**
Picture of a tree, potted plant, garden tool, packet of seeds, gardening book.

Week 2   **A time for . . . Healing**
A selection of empty pill boxes, aromatherapy oils, bandages or first aid box.

Week 3   **A time for . . . Building**
A brick, pictures of constructions, a bridge. (You could even build your own wall or bridge using any materials which are available – straws, shoeboxes, Lego, Meccano sets.)

Week 4   **A time for . . . Silence**
A candle lit during prayer time and an open Bible.

Week 5   **A time for . . . Celebrating**
Balloons, decorations, streamers, tinsel, party music.

Week 6   **A time for . . . Dancing**
Ballet shoes, pictures from magazines.

Week 7   **A time for . . . Looking Back**
Diary, calendar, old greetings cards or letters, photographs, personal artefacts from pupils.

A TIME FOR . . .

Suggested Songs/Music for 'A time for . . .' Theme

Week 1   A time for . . . Planting

'All good gifts' – from *Godspell*
'I, the Lord of sea and sky' – from *The Source*

Week 2   A time for . . . Healing

'Heal the world' – Michael Jackson
'Lay your hands' – Carey Landrey
'Deep within my heart' – Mike Anderson, from *Dance in Your Spirit*/CD
'Be still and know' – from *The Source*
'Make way, make way' – from *The Source*

Week 3   A time for . . . Building

'Don't build your house' – Karen Lafferty, from *Kidsource*
'Love can build a bridge' – Comic Relief 1995

Week 4   A time for . . . Silence

'The sound of silence' – Simon and Garfunkel
'When you say nothing at all' – Ronan Keating
'Be still, for the presence of the Lord' – from *The Source*

Week 5   A time for . . . Celebrating

'Come on and celebrate' – Patricia Morgan and Dave Bankhead, from *The Source*
'Celebration time' – Kool and the Gang
'Heaven invites you to a party' – from *The Source*

Week 6   A time for . . . Dancing

'Dance in your Spirit' – Mike Anderson, from *Dance in Your Spirit*/CD
'Down the mountain the river flows' – from *The Source*
'Teach me to dance' – from *The Source*

Week 7   A time for . . . Looking Back

'Don't look back in anger' – Oasis
'Yesterday' – The Beatles

31

The Gifts of the Spirit
A seven-week exploration

Week 1   Wisdom

Week 2   Knowledge

Week 3   Awe and Wonder

Week 4   Understanding

Week 5   Courage

Week 6   Right Judgement

Week 7   Reverence

'Prayer of the Week' Posters

Display Ideas

Suggested Songs/Music

Wisdom

Introduction

Normally when it is someone's birthday, his or her family and friends give gifts which that person usually receives with delight. But, at Christmas, because Jesus is so special, all of us celebrate his birthday by giving and receiving gifts.

Mind you, we've all had gifts that we've not really used. You can probably think of some even as recently as last Christmas. Such gifts get stored away and may not reappear until you accidentally stumble over them during a clearout.

For the next seven weeks we are going to look at seven of the gifts of the Holy Spirit. These are gifts that sometimes we have without realising it. Over the seven weeks, we are going to look at ourselves, to see if we have really received these gifts and how we might be able to use them.

Daily Prayer

Lord, you know me so very well.
Help me to know myself better.
Help me to be wise in my words and actions.
With your help I can do it.

Amen.

Pause for thought

Wisdom is about making choices, and acting on those choices.

Here is an acronym to remind you about that:

What I Say Destroys Or Mends.

- Think about what you say this week.
- What will you do?
- Destroy or mend?

Activity Here are some sayings about wisdom. Read them. Ask pupils which saying they think is the most important and useful, or get them to put them all into rank order. Then display the one chosen as most important somewhere in class for the rest of the week. You could perhaps ask a class member to write it on a larger piece of paper.

1 'It is the province of knowledge to speak, and it is the privilege of wisdom to listen.'

   Oliver Wendell Holmes (1809-94), US writer and physician.

2 'History teaches us that men and nations behave wisely once they have exhausted all other alternatives.'

   Abba Eban (b. 1915), Israeli politician. Speech, 16 Dec 1970, London.

3 'The stick and the reprimand give wisdom to children; if they have their own way, they will make their parents ashamed of them.'

   Proverbs 29:15, Hebrew Bible.

4 'Silence is as full of potential wisdom and wit as the unhewn marble of great sculpture.'

   Aldous Huxley (1894-1963), British author.

5 'Lord, grant me the courage to change the things I can change, the serenity to accept the things I can't change, and the wisdom to know the difference.'

   Traditional prayer

Scripture Solomon was the son of David, the greatest Jewish King. When Solomon was quite young he took over as king and God told him that he would give him anything he wanted. Solomon thought about this and asked for the gift of wisdom. If God offered you *anything* you wanted, what would it be?

Anyway, one day Solomon was put to the test. Two women were brought before him. They both claimed a particular baby was theirs. Solomon pondered the problem, then ordered a soldier to cut the baby in two!

Immediately one of the women shouted out that she would rather the other woman have the child than see it cut in half. Solomon knew then that the woman who shouted out must have been the mother.

Solomon did rule wisely and perhaps his greatest achievement was the building of the Temple in Jerusalem, which stood for nearly a thousand years – probably considerably longer than the Millennium Dome will last, despite the technology and materials available to us!

Knowledge

Introduction

The song 'I know him so well' is from the musical *Chess* and in the song two women are singing about the same man. They both sing that they know him so well, but actually they could be singing about different men, because one sings that all he needs is security while the other sings that what he really needs is his freedom. The irony is that really they don't know this man very well at all. They just know certain aspects of him well.

This is true about many of our relationships. We know things about a person rather than really knowing them. So how do we get to know a person? Through doing things with them, spending time with them, talking and listening to them, being with them in all sorts of situations.

What about doing some of these with Jesus this week? Have a few minutes of quiet each day. Try to picture Jesus by your side during the day. Think how he would deal with the situations you face. Talk to him in your mind. Read about him in the Gospel of Mark in a Gideon Bible, if you have one. Get to know him.

Daily Prayer

Lord, you know me so very well.
Help me to get to know others better.
Help me to use what I know for good rather than bad.
With your help I can do it.

Amen.

Pause for thought

'A little knowledge that acts is worth infinitely more than much knowledge that is idle.'

Kahlil Gibran, Lebanese poet

- Where do you stand on this?

- Are you good at putting ideas into action?

- Is there anything you know now that you should be doing something about?

Activity   Last week, one of the sayings that we discussed was:

'It is the province of knowledge to speak and the privilege of wisdom to listen.'

Here are some situations to think about and explore.

What more do you need to know?

How should you respond? (Try to get beyond the 'report it to a teacher' syndrome.)

1   You see an older pupil crying in the toilets.

2   You hear another pupil boasting that they have stolen something from a classroom.

3   You know that a friend of yours is having a difficult time at home financially. Now you hear some younger children calling them names because of their trainers.

4   You overhear a teacher talking about something personal.

5   You overhear a pupil talking about something personal.

6   You are out with a cousin of yours and are offered an 'E' for free.

Scripture   Everyone knows the story of Adam and Eve. So, answer these questions and let's see how much you know about one of the most famous pieces of literary history.

1   How did God make Adam?

2   How did God make Eve?

3   What were the two special trees in the Garden of Eden?

4   Who tempted Eve?

5   What did Eve eat that was forbidden?

6   What did Adam and Eve notice after this?

7   Who did Adam blame?

8   What happened to Adam and Eve?

Answers

1   God made Adam out of dust and then breathed into his nostrils.

2   While Adam was asleep, God took one of his ribs and covered it in flesh.

3   Tree of Life and Tree of Knowledge.

4   Serpent (note this was only a symbol of Satan – there is no mention of the devil in the text).

5   Fruit from the Tree of Knowledge (not an apple).

6   They were naked.

7   Adam blamed Eve.

8   They were expelled from the Garden of Eden – so they could not eat from the Tree of Life, which meant that one day they would die.

Awe and Wonder

Introduction

In our increasingly technological, digital and conspicuous consumer society, it is easy to become blasé about the world. For example, it is commonplace for people to fly to other countries. At the beginning of the last century, such an idea would have been inconceivable. It is now possible to communicate with people on the other side of the world by means of telephones and computers. Just a few decades ago this would have seemed ridiculous. Humans have even stood on the moon! All wonderful achievements!

And yet, truly wonderful moments may come not through technology but through other people. The first time you fall in love is wonderful. You can be filled with wonder when you see the miracle of a little baby. When someone achieves something in spite of terrible difficulties – you can be awestruck.

This week, try to focus on what is wonderful in the people around you. Each of us is a miracle – a wonder to be appreciated. Let's enjoy each other – every single one of us made in the image of God. (It makes you realise what a sense of humour God must have.) So, go on, look in the mirror each morning this week and say to yourself – 'I am the pinnacle of God's creative power! I'm awesome!'

Daily Prayer

Lord, you know me so very well.
Help me to appreciate myself.
Help me to appreciate the wonder of everyone I meet.
With your help I can do it.

Amen.

Pause for Thought

'What is this life if, full of care,
we have no time to stand and stare?'

William Davies (1871-1940)

Davies was an interesting character who left the UK on a cattle ship to hitch-hike through America. He had to have a leg amputated after he jumped off a train in Canada. He returned to England and slept rough, making his living as a street singer. His poem 'Leisure' was voted fourteenth in the 'Nation's Favourite Poems' poll on National Poetry Day, 1995.

Activity

The Seven Wonders of the Ancient World were:

- the Pyramids
- the Hanging Gardens of Babylon
- the Mausoleum at Halicarnassus
- the Temple to the goddess Artemis at Ephesus
- the Colossus of Rhodes
- the Statue of Zeus by Phidias
- the Pharos (lighthouse) at Alexandria.

All of them were made by humans, using their God-given talents. Only the Pyramids of the above remain.

Try to come up with your own list of seven modern wonders of the world. (Don't limit this to buildings. You can include any human achievement over the last century, e.g. going to the moon, breaking the speed of sound, discovery of penicillin, etc.)

Then try to come up with seven natural wonders of the world. (You can include mountains, rivers, animals, insects, etc.)

Finally try to make a list of your seven human wonders of the world. (These should be the seven people you think are most wonderful, whether famous or seemingly ordinary.)

Scripture

O Lord, our Lord, your greatness is seen in all the world! When I look at the sky, which you have made, at the moon and the stars, which you set in their places – compared to them, what are human beings, that you think of them and care for them?

Yet you appointed them rulers over everything you made; you placed them over all creation: sheep and cattle, and the wild animals too; the birds and the fish and the creatures in the seas.

Psalm 8

Nowadays, telescopes and satellites can reveal the most accurate and amazing information about the stars. Astronomers tell us that some stars we see simply don't exist anymore; that – because they are so far away – we see them as they were millions of years ago. It takes the light from them that long to travel to us (even at 186,000 miles per second!)

The words of the Psalm above – originally a song written possibly by King David – express the writer's wonder at the stars and moon. Although written 3,000 years ago, the words still mean something today. We do have a responsibility to the world, to the environment, to the animals and to each other. Have a look at the stars this week – realise how vast the universe is. Be mindful of your place in it.

Understanding

Introduction

During this theme we have been looking at the gifts of the Holy Spirit. So far, we've thought about Wisdom, Knowledge, and Awe and Wonder. The next gift is that of Understanding. So many of the problems in the world today are caused by lack of understanding – problems on a global scale, like the debt crisis facing many poor nations; problems on a much more personal level – perhaps between classmates and work colleagues. Maybe you've had an experience like this when you feel that someone just doesn't understand you and yet makes judgements which affect you.

Of course, understanding is very much a two-way process, which underlines the importance of communication. We can't expect people to understand us if we don't take opportunities to express ourselves. Mind you, neither can we absolve ourselves of the responsibility to listen to others. Too often, we can be so busy expressing how we feel that we don't listen carefully enough to others. Have you ever been in a conversation or argument when, as soon as you've said something, you start formulating what you are going to say next – rather than listen to what the other person is saying?

This week, the challenge is to make a more conscious effort to listen and understand.

Daily Prayer

Lord, you know me so very well.
Help me to understand my own feelings and those of others.
Help me to understand how you want me to live my life.
With your help I can make a difference.

Amen.

Pause for Thought

'If you don't understand yourself you don't understand anybody else.'

Nikki Giovanni (1971), American poet.

- Do you sometimes do things – then wonder why you did them?
- Do you sometimes say things – that you wish you hadn't said?
- Do you sometimes wish you understood yourself more?

If you answer 'YES' to these questions – welcome to the human race!

Activity

Here is a list of anagrams. Each word fits in the blank in the following sentence.

.... **experiences can develop our understanding.**

1	SUUUALN	(Unusual)
2	ENW	(New)
3	FREDENTIF	(Different)
4	TENXCIGI	(Exciting)
5	SHERGREFIN	(Refreshing)
6	ASD	(Sad)
7	STINGET	(Testing)
8	RATSICIT	(Artistic)
9	VAINGEET	(Negative)
10.	SEVERID	(Diverse)
11	GRISTEENTIN	(Interesting)
12	RACEYNESS	(Necessary)
13	GIGLUNERL	(Gruelling)

Try and work them out. The initial letters of the first words spell an appropriate word. Comprende?

Scripture

I want you to be happy, always happy in the Lord; I repeat, what I want is your happiness. Be tolerant with everyone – the Lord is very near. There is no need to worry; but if there is anything you need, pray for it – and that peace of God, which is so much greater than we can understand, will guard your hearts and thoughts.

St. Paul's Letter to the Philippians 4:4-7

St. Paul wrote this letter about 25 years after the death of Jesus. This was before any of the Gospels were written and, at the time, Paul was under arrest for telling people about Jesus. In another part of this letter, Paul warns the early followers of Jesus that certain enemies are out to get them. He also wrote about two of the followers of Jesus who were at each other's throats, begging them to come to some agreement. It seems these were troubled times. But what was Paul's advice? He said there was no need to worry and that prayer was the answer; that prayer would bring peace, a peace beyond human understanding!

Maybe some of his words apply to you today. Certainly, it is good to hear that we should be looking for happiness in our lives. So often, people think religion is about rules and regulations which restrict freedom and impose discipline. On the contrary – whatever we live our lives by should bring us happiness, contentment and fun!

Courage

Introduction

There is a common misconception that brave people feel no fear. This is ridiculous. After all, if you are not frightened of something, you have no need to be brave.

Modern-day Christians have a great heritage of courage: from Jesus himself, to the early martyrs, right up to recent times and people like Maximilian Kolbe, Oscar Romero and Martin Luther King.

Fortunately, the number of people called to such amazingly courageous acts of faith are few, but we are all called to take courage in our own situation: in school, at home, in society; to stand up and be counted as witnesses to Jesus. For example, do you have the courage to stand up for those who are given a hard time by bullies who intimidate, ridicule and humiliate? Courage costs, because you can end up a victim too! But maybe your example will make the difference and turn the tide against those who seek to make life a misery for others.

Daily Prayer

Lord, you know me so very well.
Help me to cope with fear – fear of being left out,
fear of being laughed at, fear of disappointing others.
Help me to have the courage to do what is right –
even if it is unpopular.
With your help I can do it.

Amen.

Pause for Thought

'I'm very brave generally, only today I happen to have a headache.'

Tweedledum in *Alice Through the Looking Glass* by Lewis Carroll

- Can you relate to this?

- What do you use as excuses for wimping out when you should show courage?

- Is there some area of your life in which you need to take courage?

Ask God to help!

43

Activity

Arachnophobia was a pretty scary film about deadly spiders invading a town in America. A 'phobia' is an irrational fear of something. Here are some – can you find out what they are?

CLAUSTROPHOBIA	(fear of enclosed spaces)
ASTRAPHOBIA	(fear of lightning)
TRISKAIDEKAPHOBIA	(fear of the number 13)
POGONOPHOBIA	(fear of beards)
NYCTOPHOBIA	(fear of the night)
XENOPHOBIA	(fear of foreigners)
CAINOTOPHOBIA	(fear of anything new)
ZOOPHOBIA	(fear of animals)
AILUROPHOBIA	(fear of cats)
MONOPHOBIA	(fear of being alone)

One of the ways to overcome these phobias is 'aversion therapy'. For instance, arachnophobics will go through small steps leading up to actually holding a spider. It can be very successful.

Are there any small steps you could take to overcoming your fears?

Scripture

Between three and six o'clock in the morning Jesus came to the disciples, walking on the water. When they saw him walking on the water, they were terrified. 'It's a ghost!' they said, and screamed with fear. Jesus spoke to them at once. 'Courage!' he said. 'It is I. Don't be afraid!'

Then Peter spoke up: 'Lord, if it is really you, order me to come out on the water to you.'

'Come!' answered Jesus. So Peter got out of the boat and started walking on the water to Jesus. But when he noticed the strong wind, he was afraid and started to sink down in the water. 'Save me, Lord!' he cried.

Matthew 14

In this story, we see how Peter has the courage to leave the relative safety of the boat. But there is more to this than meets the eye. Water is generally used in our society as a symbol of cleanliness and goodness, because it is essential for life. However, at the time of Jesus water had two meanings: one was 'goodness', the other 'evil', because at various points in their history, the Jews had had crops destroyed by floods.

So, the story of Jesus walking on the water symbolises Jesus' power over evil and we, like Peter, are called to take courage in the battle against the evil in our own world. So, take courage and be confident that Jesus will help you just as he helped Peter.

Right Judgement

Introduction

The gift we are looking at this week is Right Judgement. In 1999, at the Brit Awards, Robbie Williams was judged by members of the music industry to be Best Male Artist, to have sung the Best Single – 'Angels' – and to have been in the Best Video – Millennium. For each of these he received a statuette. Maybe you thought that someone else should have won one or more of these awards, but, like it or not, the records show that, according to the music industry, Robbie Williams won.

You see the thing that makes a judgement different from an everyday choice is that a judgement has an air of finality about it. In the case of the Brit Awards the judgements from previous years can be looked up. They are a snapshot in time of particular judgements – they cannot be changed.

When a defendant in court is judged, that judgement is a formal declaration of guilt or innocence after all the evidence available has been considered. Our justice system allows people to appeal against judgements but eventually the opportunities to appeal run out and a final judgement is made.

This week, we are thinking about the gift of right judgement. We need to ask ourselves how we make judgements about other people. Do we judge them on the basis of lots of evidence or do we judge them merely on what others say about them? Do we really get to know them before we sentence them by the way we treat them? Do we consider and look for their good points as well as what we believe to be their bad points? Maybe you've been misjudged in the past. Try to remember how it felt and use that to help you in judging others fairly.

Daily Prayer

Lord, you know me so very well.
Help me to judge others fairly.
Help me to look for good in others.
Help me to reserve judgement rather than condemn.
With your help I can do it.
Amen.

Pause for Thought

'I have a dream today that one day my children will live in a nation where they will not be judged by the colour of their skin but by the content of their character.'

Martin Luther King (1929-68)

- Do you judge by the colour of skin?
- What is your stereotype of Chinese people?
- What is your stereotype of black people?
- What is your stereotype of Pakistani people?
- Do you have prejudices?
- What is your stereotype of white people?

Activity   Make your own judgements as a class about the following categories:

- Best single (ever!)
- Best pop group (ever!)
- Person most likely to make England's football team into world champions
- Person most likely to make the world a better place
- Best role model for young men
- Best role model for young women
- Best maxim for life
- Most important event in human history

Why not compare them to the judgements of some of the other classes in school?

Scripture   *Do not judge others, so that God will not judge you, for God will judge you in the same way as you judge others, and he will apply to you the same rules you apply to others.*

Why, then, do you look at the speck in your brother's eye, and pay no attention to the log in your own eye? How dare you say to your brother, 'Please, let me take that speck out of your eye,' when you have a log in your own eye? You hypocrite! First take the log out of your own eye, and then you will be able to see clearly to take the speck out of your brother's eye.

Matthew 7:1-5

This forms part of the Sermon on the Mount – a collection of Jesus' teachings – which contains much humour. Look at the passage above and try to imagine how Jesus might have said it.

He uses this image of someone with a plank in his eye trying to get a speck of dust out of someone else's eye. Can you picture the absurdity of it? In other parts of the Sermon on the Mount Jesus exaggerates in order to make a point – but there is always a point!

In this case, Jesus is basically reiterating part of the prayer that he taught his followers. Can you work out which line?

Reverence

Introduction

The final gift of the Holy Spirit that we are considering in this series is Reverence. This is about treating God, ourselves and others with honour or respect. Reverence is very much part of our culture and tradition in this country.

Our judicial system has a formal way of expressing reverence – we address the judge as 'Your Honour'. In the House of Commons, members of Parliament address each other as 'The Right Honourable Member' – although they very often proceed to treat each other with less than respect. In church vicars are formally addressed as 'Reverend'. In school, pupils show respect by addressing their teachers appropriately.

But reverence is not something to be afforded just to a select few – judges, MPs, clergy or teachers. No, reverence is about treating everyone with respect and treating everyone as if they matter to us. Jesus was quite revolutionary in this regard. His story is full of instances where he treats outcasts with respect. So, this week, let's try to walk in his footsteps and respect others. That's not to say we have to bow to people, but we can show reverence by listening to others. We can show reverence by not belittling others because they are different. We can show reverence by appreciating that they are just as important to God as we are.

Daily Prayer

Lord, you know me so very well.
Help me to appreciate this world.
Help me to honour those who care for me.
Help me to respect others even when I find them difficult.
With your help I can do it.
Amen.

Pause for thought

'We have not the reverent feeling for the rainbow that a savage has, because we know how it is made.'
Mark Twain (1835-1910)

- Can you enjoy the beauty of a rainbow?
- Does music touch your emotions?
- Can you look at the moon and still be impressed?

Or are you so sophisticated that you find no joy in them?

Activity

Last week, we made judgements about various categories. Here are just a selection of answers given by pupils in another school in 1999. Can you respect their judgements? Reverence is about accepting and valuing others' viewpoints, whether we agree with them or not.

- Best single (ever!): nominations included 'Millennium', 'Baby One More Time', 'Angels', 'Feed The World', 'Bohemian Rhapsody', 'Believe'.

- Best pop group (ever!): nominations included Steps, Oasis, The Beatles, and Five.

- Person most likely to make England's football team into world champions: nominations included Kevin Keegan, Terry Venables and Michael Owen.

- Person most likely to make the world a better place: nominations included Tony Blair, each one of us, Martin Luther King, Princess Diana, Michael Jackson, Muhammad Ali.

- Best role model for young men: nominations included Michael Owen, Cane, Johnny Vaughan and Winnie the Pooh. (The class who nominated Winnie the Pooh reckoned he was always cheerful, always took care of others – especially Piglet – and was pretty unmaterialistic, because the only thing he wanted was honey!)

- Best role model for young women: nominations included Princess Diana, Celine Dion, Mother Teresa, Billie, Britney Spears, Madonna, girls' mums.

- Most important event in human history: nominations included the end of World War II and the birth of Jesus.

Scripture

Jesus was having a meal in Levi's house. A large number of tax collectors and other outcasts were following Jesus, and many of them joined him and his disciples at the table. Some teachers of the Law, who were Pharisees, saw that Jesus was eating with these outcasts and tax collectors, so they asked his disciples, 'Why does he eat with such people?' Jesus heard them and answered, 'People who are well do not need a doctor, but only those who are sick. I have not come to call respectable people, but outcasts.'

Mark 2:15-18

Jesus respected everyone. He touched lepers – the outcasts of society in those days. (Maybe sometimes you feel left out by others.) He loved the disabled. (Maybe sometimes you feel disabled or inadequate in some way.) He spoke up for sinners. (Maybe sometimes you choose to do wrong.) Jesus seemed to be able to appreciate everyone as an individual. He treated them with respect and they loved him. He loves us too, even though we might not deserve it. So, we're called to follow the example of Jesus. Not easy? Certainly! Inconvenient? Definitely! Desirable? Absolutely!

Prayer

Lord, you know me so very well.

Help me to know myself better.

Help me to be wise in my words and actions.

With your help I can do it.

Amen.

Wissdom

Prayer

Lord, you know me so very well.

Help me to get to know others better.

Help me to use what I know for good rather than bad.

With your help I can do it.

Amen.

Knowledge

Prayer

Lord, you know me so very well.

Help me to appreciate myself.

Help me to appreciate the wonder

of everyone I meet.

With your help I can do it.

Amen.

Awe and Wonder

Prayer

Lord, you know me so very well.

Help me to understand my own feelings and those of others.

Help me to understand how you want me to live my life.

With your help I can make a difference.

Amen.

Understanding

Prayer

Lord, you know me so very well.

Help me to cope with fear –

fear of being left out,

fear of being laughed at,

fear of disappointing others.

Help me to have the courage to do what is right –

even if it is unpopular.

With your help I can do it.

Amen.

Courage

Prayer

Lord, you know me so very well.

Help me to judge others fairly.

Help me to look for good in others.

Help me to reserve judgement

rather than condemn.

With your help I can do it.

Amen.

Right Judgement

Prayer

Lord, you know me so very well.

Help me to appreciate this world.

Help me to honour those who care for me.

Help me to respect others

even when I find them difficult.

With your help I can do it.

Amen.

Reverence

Display Idea for 'Gifts of the Spirit' Theme

A good central image for display would be a dove or cross from around which the prayer for each week is displayed.

Gifts of the Spirit

Suggested Songs/Music for 'Gifts of the Spirit' Theme

Week 1: Wisdom

'Never forget' – Take That

'Father and son' – Boyzone or Cat Stevens

Week 2: Knowledge

'I know him so well' – Elaine Page and Barbara Dickson

'Now I know what love is' – Mike Anderson, from *Dance in Your Spirit*/CD

Week 3: Awe and Wonder

'What a wonderful world' – Louis Armstrong or Alison Moyet

'Shine, Jesus, shine' – Graham Kendrick, from *The Source*

'Lord of life' – Mike Anderson, from *Dance in Your Spirit*/CD

'Your love's greater' – Mike Anderson, from *Dance in Your Spirit*/CD

Week 4: Understanding

'We can work it out' – The Beatles

'Some day we'll know' – New Radicals

'Jesus Christ, I think upon your sacrifice' – from *The Source*

Week 5: Courage

'When the going gets tough' – Boyzone

'Be bold, be strong' – from *The Source*

Week 6: Right Judgement

'The kingdom of heaven' – Mike Anderson, from *Dance in Your Spirit*/CD

Week 7: Reverence

'Be still, for the presence of the Lord' – David J. Evans, from *The Source*

'Majesty' – from *The Source*

'Heaven from here' – Robbie Williams

Hollywood Films

A four-week series

Week 1: Forrest Gump

Week 2: Gone with the Wind

Week 3: The Wizard of Oz

Week 4: Star Wars

'Prayer of the Week' Posters

Display Ideas

Suggested Songs/Music

FORREST GUMP

Introduction

Over the next four weeks we are going to be following a series on films during Sacred Time. We'll also be looking at the lives of some saints! But the film for this week is *Forrest Gump*.

This Oscar-winning film follows the life of Forrest Gump – someone who was not overly blessed in the brains department – and his encounters with famous people and events in recent history. He meets up with and influences Elvis. He fights in the Vietnam War, becoming a hero. He loves and nurses his childhood sweetheart, Jenny.

Although a simpleton, Forrest is a truly good man who responds positively to every situation he faces, and somehow discovers that he has the gifts and strength of character to help him come through the bad times.

We can all learn from his positive attitude to life.

Famous Words

'Life is like a box of chocolates – you never know what you're going to get!'

Sometimes in life we get surprises and sometimes shocks!

Reflect on your own life and think about times when you got a lovely surprise. Share these moments with others in your class.

Daily Prayer

Lord God,
help us to see the good in others;
help us to speak words which encourage;
help us to smile more.
Amen.

60

Activity

Getting a box of chocolates is a treat. Giving someone a box of chocolates is a symbol of affection and love.

1 Think about your three favourite chocolates. You could do a class survey.

2 Now, imagine life is like a box of chocolates. The chocolates are all surprises which would make life better for the person you give them to. Think of someone special in your life and think about the three surprises you would like them to have if you could arrange it. For example, you might want them to have good health; you might want them to have the chance to visit someone; you might want them to have success in a job.

3 Now, think about the three surprises you would like yourself – but don't just think about money and what that can bring. There are other far more important things which can make your life happier.

4 Finally, if you were a chocolate, what do think you would be?

   • Are you quite hard of heart on the inside but all sweetness and light on the outside – a hazelnut swirl?

   • Do you make life difficult for others – a toffee chew?

   • Do you try to be hard on the outside, but really you're quite gentle and soft on the inside – a chocolate eclair?

   • What kind of chocolate would your friends be?

Gone With The Wind

Introduction

Gone with the Wind is an amazing movie. It was the biggest and most successful movie of its time.

Based on the novel by Margaret Mitchell, it follows the life of Scarlett O'Hara, a beautiful but manipulative girl, through the years before, during and after the American Civil War.

Scarlett had everything in life that some people regard as essential to happiness – wealth, looks and influence. However, Scarlett was one of those people who are rarely happy with what they have. Maybe you know someone like that.

Eventually, she lost the man she loved – Rhett Butler – but she refused to be crushed and downhearted. While we might not share her values, we can still admire her spirit.

Famous Words

'After all, tomorrow is another day!'

At the end of the film Scarlett O'Hara speaks these words. Sometimes it's easy to dwell on what has happened in the past and it can be hard to put the bad things behind us.

Reflect on your life – do you live in the past? If you do, take courage – don't forget about the past, but don't let it stop you being the best you can be.

Daily Prayer

Lord God,

help us to see that we can't change what has happened;

help us to see how we can put things right for the future;

help us to be the best we can be.

Amen.

HOLLYWOOD FILMS: WEEK 2

Activity

The famous last words of Scarlett O'Hara can help us focus on tomorrow. Have a go at writing a poem, each line of which starts with the letters in the word **TOMORROW**.

For example:

Truthful

Open

Mediating

Organised

Responsible

Reasonable

One day can make a difference

When will I be what I can be?

or

Trusting

Others?

Many times I've done that

Only to be

Rejected and hurt.

Running away isn't the answer

Only I don't want to be hurt again.

Will I ever trust someone else again? Maybe!

THE WIZARD OF OZ

Introduction

The *Wizard of Oz* was released in 1939 and starred Judy Garland. It was the first major studio film released in colour!

It's really the story of four characters each looking for something different. Dorothy is looking for the Wizard of Oz, who can take her back to her home town – Kansas – from which she has been taken by a twister!

On her journey on the Yellow Brick Road to the Emerald City, she meets the Scarecrow, the Tin Man and the Cowardly Lion. They each decide they will accompany her so that they can ask the Wizard to help them. The Scarecrow wants a brain, the Tin Man wants a heart and the Cowardly Lion wants some courage!

They have many adventures together and eventually realise that each of them already has what they were looking for. They just didn't realise how gifted they were because they hadn't used these gifts before.

This week, let's think about our own God-given gifts – some of which may be under-used!

Famous Words

'If I only had a . . .'

The Scarecrow kept saying, 'If I only had a brain!' The Tin Man kept saying, 'If I only had a heart!' The Cowardly Lion kept saying, 'If I only had some courage!'

What would the *'If only I had . . .'* be in your life as regards:

   (a) material things   (b) personal qualities

Do you have control over either of these?

Are you happy with what you have got and what you are?

Daily Prayer

Lord God,

help us to see that we are all gifted;

help us to use our gifts;

help us to encourage others to use their gifts.

    Amen.

Activity

In the film, Dorothy goes in search of the Wizard of Oz whose help she needs. She gets to the Emerald City and has a 'one 2 one' with him to find out how to get back to Kansas.

You've all seen the adverts for having a 'one 2 one' with famous people, such as Ian Wright with Martin Luther King and Chris Evans.

Who would you like to have a 'one 2 one' with, and why? If you could only ask them three questions, what would they be?

Now, imagine having a 'one 2 one' with Jesus. What three questions would you ask?

Share your ideas with others near you or role-play the 'one 2 one' with someone taking on the roles of Jesus and your other heroes.

STAR WARS

Introduction

Recently the first episode of *Star Wars* was released, somewhat strangely after episodes 4, 5 and 6!

When you strip the *Star Wars* saga of all the special effects, what you get is basically a story of an ongoing battle between good and evil. In episode 4, Obi-wan Kenobi is the essence of all that is good and Darth Vader is the personification of all that is evil.

The same sort of struggles have been going on throughout the world for thousands of years. Unfortunately, people like Darth Vader have always existed. You need only consider the Holocaust, in which six million Jews were exterminated, to realise this is true.

However, let's not lose sight of the fact that there is so much good in the world, too. Most people do choose good rather than evil most of the time and sometimes there are heroic examples of this – like Maximilian Kolbe, the priest who gave his life to save another's in the Holocaust. This week, let's try be more aware of the choices we face, and make good ones!

Famous Words

'The force be with you!'

These were the words spoken by Obi-wan Kenobi, which Luke Skywalker remembered when he needed help.

Can you remember any words that people have spoken to you which you remember particularly well?

Has anyone ever said just the right thing for you at just the right time?

Is it just possible that God helped them to say these words?

Daily Prayer

Lord Jesus,
you promised you would always be with us.
Help us to be more aware of your presence
in our lives.
Amen.

Activity

'The force be with you!' are words spoken by Jedi knights. They are the words which inspire Luke to continue his struggle even when all seems lost.

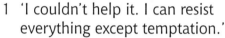

Here are some other famous words. See if you can match them with the people below.

1 'I couldn't help it. I can resist everything except temptation.'
2 'You see but do not observe.'
3 'If I have seen further it is by standing on the shoulders of giants!'
4 'Come to me all you who labour and are heavily burdened. I will give you rest.'
5 'Love is blind.'

a Jesus
b Oscar Wilde (playwright and wit)
c Isaac Newton (scientist)
d Sherlock Holmes
   (fictional detective created by Sir Arthur Conan Doyle)
e William Shakespeare (playwright)

Answers: 1b, 2d, 3c, 4a, 5e

Talk about what each means. Which do you like best? If there were a phrase that you could be remembered for, what would it be?

The words of Jesus are recorded in the Gospels. Make a list of some of the sayings of Jesus that you can remember.

FORREST GUMP

Famous Words

'Life is like a box of chocolates – you never know what you're going to get!'

Daily Prayer

Lord God,

help us to see

the good in others;

help us to speak words

which encourage;

help us to smile more.

Amen.

Gone with the Wind

Famous Words

'After all, tomorrow is another day!'

Daily Prayer

Lord God,

help us to see that we can't change what has happened;

help us to see how we can put things right for the future;

help us to be the best we can be.

Amen.

The Wizard Of Oz

Famous Words

'If I only had a . . .'

Daily Prayer

Lord God,

help us to see that we are all gifted;

help us to use our gifts;

help us to encourage others to use their gifts.

Amen.

STAR WARS

HOLLYWOOD

Famous Words

'The force be with you!'

Daily Prayer

Lord Jesus,
you promised you would
always be with us.
Help us to be more aware
of your presence in our
lives.
Amen.

Display Idea for 'Hollywood Films' Theme

Display the 'Daily Prayer' and 'Famous Words' sheets in the beams of drawings of spot/laser lights or on images of clapperboards.

Suggested Songs/Music for 'Hollywood Films' Theme

Week 1: Forrest Gump

'Around the world' – Nat King Cole

'Never forget' – Take That

'I'll be there for you' – The Rembrandts (Theme from *Friends*)

Week 2: Gone with the Wind

'Brand new start' – Paul Weller

'Could we start again, please?' – from *Jesus Christ Superstar*

Week 3: The Wizard of Oz

'Somewhere over the rainbow' – Judy Garland

'When the going gets tough' – Boyzone

'At every end there's a beginning' – Gladys Knight and the Pips

Week 4: Star Wars

Star Wars theme by John Williams

'Never forget' – Take That

'When you wish upon a star' – from *Pinocchio*

Plays of Shakespeare

A four-week series

Week 1: Much Ado About Nothing

Week 2: The Tempest

Week 3: Romeo and Juliet

Week 4: A Midsummer Night's Dream

'Prayer of the Week' Posters

Display Ideas

Suggested Songs/Music

Much Ado About Nothing

Introduction

One of the most successful films of recent years has been *Shakespeare In Love*. Over the next four weeks we will be looking at some of the titles of his plays, starting with *Much Ado About Nothing*.

This is a comedy in which the two main characters – Beatrice and Benedick – spend most of the time bickering and badmouthing each other. Eventually they realise that they actually love each other and they form an unlikely alliance to help another couple get married. Finally, after various trials and tribulations, there is a happy ending and everyone realises that their earlier difficulties are not that significant after all.

How true that is for us! We do sometimes face major problems in our lives. However insurmountable many of today's problems might seem, we will be able to look back in the years ahead and realise they were 'much ado about nothing'.

Daily Prayer

Lord – help me to accept the things I can't change.
Lord – give me the courage to change the things I can change.
And, above all, Lord –
give me the wisdom to know the difference.

Amen.

From Bard to Verse

'I do love nothing in the world so well as you:
is that not strange?'

Benedick to Beatrice in Act 4, Scene 1

Isn't it strange too that Jesus loves each of us?

No matter what we do!

No matter what we say!

No matter if we try to shut him out of our lives!

In fact, Jesus loves us so much that he opened his arms to hug us and we nailed them to a cross.

77

Activity

Here is a list of things that affect our lives in some way. Rewrite the list in rank order of their importance to you. (Most important at the top!) Then rewrite them in the order you think Bill Gates (the world's richest man) might place them. Finally, rewrite them in the order that Jesus might put them.

Being fashionable
Being rich
Being happy
Being generous
Being popular
Being successful
Being respected
Being loved

Compare the lists. If they are different, why are they different?

Scripture

Jesus said to them:

Why worry about clothes? Look how the wild flowers grow: they do not work or make clothes for themselves. But I tell you that not even King Solomon with all his wealth had clothes as beautiful as one of these flowers.

So do not worry about tomorrow; it will have enough worries of its own. There is no need to add to the troubles each day brings.

Matthew 6:28-29, 34

Do you get worried about clothes? Maybe you think or say things like:

- I could do with another pair of trainers
- That Nike jacket is last year's style
- I need a new Helly-Hansen
- I can't wear that – it isn't in fashion
- My mates'll laugh at me

Look at a TV news item about refugees or victims of natural disasters! Do you think they're bothered by such ideas?

If you're going to worry – worry about important things!

The Tempest

Introduction

This week's play starts with a shipwreck. One of the survivors is Ferdinand, a good-looking prince, who is washed up on an island inhabited by Prospero and his beautiful daughter Miranda.

The inevitable happens and the two young people fall in love. However, Prospero puts obstacles in their way. There are other storms along the way as Prospero, the rightful Duke of Milan, encounters his brother who usurped him. There is a plot against the life of Ferdinand's father, the King of Naples; and Caliban (Prospero's slave) and some drunken sailors try to get the better of Prospero.

However, the heroes survive the stormy goings on and they all live happily ever after. This week, let's consider the storms in our lives and maybe how we cause storms for other people.

Daily Prayer

Just as you calmed the wind
and walked upon the sea,
conquer, my living Lord,
the storms that threaten me.

Amen.

From Bard to Verse

'How many goodly creatures are there here!
How beauteous mankind is!
O brave new world, that hath such people in't.'

Miranda in Act 5, Scene 1.

Who are the *goodly creatures* in your life?

* the people who make you happy?

* the people who help you overcome your storms?

* the people who make you feel loved and valued?

Enjoy such people! Enjoy this brave new world that has so much good in it! Do your bit towards making it even better!

79

Activity

In Act 1, Scene 2, Ferdinand, who has just survived the shipwreck, wanders about the island and he hears a beautiful song, sung by the fairy, Ariel. Ferdinand says:

This music crept by me upon the waters,
allaying both their fury, and my passion, with its sweet air.

You've probably got some songs that soothe you and help you to stay calm. Talk about them and come up with a list of all-time 'soothers'. Then choose the three most soothing – the three most likely to keep you calm in times of trouble.

Here are a few to start you off:

- 'Perfect day' (various artists)
- 'Bridge over troubled waters' – Simon and Garfunkel
- 'I'll be there for you' – The Rembrandts (theme from *Friends*)
- 'Do not be afraid' (hymn)

Why not bring one in sometime this week and play it in prayer time?

Scripture

Suddenly a strong wind blew up, and the waves began to spill over into the boat, so that it was about to sink. Jesus was in the back of the boat, asleep. The disciples woke him up and said, 'Teacher, don't you care that we are about to die?' Jesus stood up and commanded the wind, 'Be quiet!' and he said to the waves, 'Be still!' The wind died down, and there was a great calm.

Then Jesus said to his disciples, 'Why are you frightened? Have you still no faith?' But they were terribly afraid and said to one another, 'Who is this man?'

Mark 4:36-41

This is a great story but isn't it strange that:

- Jesus managed to stay asleep in the midst of this tempest
- Jesus asked the disciples why they were frightened (wasn't it obvious?)
- Jesus told the disciples off for their lack of faith
- by the end of the story the disciples are more frightened than ever!

The question they asked remains relevant for us: *Who is this man, Jesus?* What does he mean to us?

Romeo and Juliet

Introduction

This is one of the most famous pieces of world literature. Its very title is so ingrained in our culture that to mention it evokes images of love. Even those who have neither seen nor read the play know that Romeo and Juliet were lovers.

Just a few years ago, a film was made of the play, starring none other than Leonardo Di Caprio. The opening of the film powerfully brings the story to life as members of the enemy households – the Montagues and Capulets – fight it out at a petrol station!

Amidst the anger, antagonism and hatred, Romeo and Juliet fall in love. However, their plan to live happily ever after ends tragically. An important letter is undelivered, misunderstanding ensues, and Romeo and Juliet both die. Yet their warring families come together in their grief and make a fresh start with each other. Love conquers all!

Daily Prayer

Put love in our hearts, Lord Jesus:
love for you, love for those around us,
love for those we find it hard to like.

Amen.

From Bard to Verse

'Seal up the mouth of outrage for a while,
till we can clear these ambiguities.'

Escalus, the Prince of Verona, in Act 5, Scene 3

(These words are spoken to members of the warring families upon their discovery of the dead couple.)

- Do you ever need to seal your mouth?
- Have you ever hurt someone by what you've said?
- Have you ever made things worse in a relationship by what you've said?
- Have you ever 'opened you mouth and put your foot in it', as it were?

81

Activity

There used to be a cartoon series in the daily papers entitled: 'Love is . . .' It portrayed two characters and the way they showed their love for each other in a sometimes very down-to-earth way. For example: 'Love is . . . doing the washing up while there are still clean plates in the cupboard' or 'Love is . . . giving her flowers just because you love her'.

Here is a series of statements about love:

Love is patient and kind;
it is not jealous or conceited or proud;
love is not ill-mannered or selfish or irritable;
love does not keep a record of wrongs;
love is not happy with evil, but is happy with the truth.
Love never gives up.

So how good are you at love – real love; not romantic, slushy love, but real down-to-earth love? Here is the same passage as before – but instead of 'love' the word 'I' is inserted. Count up as this is read; just how many of these phrases describe you? There are 12 in all:

I am (1) patient and (2) kind;
I am (3) not jealous, (4) not conceited, and (5) not proud;
I am (6) not ill-mannered, (7) not selfish, and (8) not irritable;
I (9) don't keep a record of wrongs;
I am (10) not happy with evil, but I am (11) happy with the truth.
I (12) never give up.

Ratings:
10-12 = very good   7-9 = average   1-6 = room for improvement

Scripture

Jesus said to them: 'My children, I shall not be with you very much longer. And now I give you a new commandment: love one another. As I have loved you, so you must love one another. If you have love for one another, then everyone will know that you are my disciples.'

John 13:33-35

At the Last Supper, Jesus gave his friends this new commandment. Not only does it replace the Ten Commandments, it also does away with the need for any other laws! Every other law could be done away with if everyone in the world could follow this one commandment to 'love one another'.

Maybe you can think of some laws that we just wouldn't need if everyone did love one another?

A Midsummer Night's Dream

Introduction

This is a fabulous play. It's got intrigue, love, comedy, a play within a play, magic potions, fairies, a wedding – and a happy ending!

In short, Theseus loves Hippolyta and Hippolyta loves Theseus. They are getting married – simple! Oberon loves Titania but they have a pretty on-off kind of relationship and it's more off than on for most of the play. Meanwhile Helena fancies Demetrius but Demetrius fancies Hermia. Lysander also fancies Hermia and fortunately for Lysander – Hermia fancies him and not Demetrius. Nobody fancies Helena – aah!

Confused? This is just the start! It makes *Eastenders* seem like *Postman Pat*. Eventually, though, everyone's dream comes true! This week we think about our dreams and how we can turn them into reality.

Daily Prayer

**Lord, the kingdom of heaven is a place
where there are no more tears,
no more pain and no more suffering.
Help us to work towards making this vision a reality
here and now.**

Amen.

From Bard to Verse

'The course of true love never did run smooth.'

Lysander (who fancies Hermia, remember?), Act 1, Scene 1.

Turning your dreams into reality is not something that necessarily comes easily. You have to work at it!

- Do you have the 'stickability' and determination to make your dreams a reality?

- Will you let disappointments put you off?

- Do you ever help others to make their dreams into reality?

83

Activity

Martin Luther King once said:

'I have a dream today that one day my children will live in a nation where they will not be judged by the colour of their skin but by the content of their character.'

You can look it up on most computer encyclopaedias and listen to the speech. It's very emotional.

What are your dreams for this nation and this world?

Work together to draft your own paragraph which starts:
'We have a dream today that one day our children will live in a *nation* . . .'
Now draft a paragraph that starts:
'We have a dream today that one day our children will live in a *world* . . .'

Issues you might like to consider are war, ethnic cleansing, starvation, world debt, injustice, torture.

Scripture

A man suffering from leprosy came to Jesus, knelt down, and begged him for help. 'If you want to,' he said, 'you can make me clean.'

Jesus was filled with pity, and stretched out his hand and touched him. 'I do want to,' he answered. 'Be clean!' At once the disease left the man, and he was clean.

Mark 1:40-42

In this week's play a magic potion is used on various characters as they sleep. When they wake the potion makes them love the first person they see – sometimes with hilarious results.

Jesus, however, did not need a magic potion to love people. Even the wretched leper who would have been disfigured, smelly and pretty unattractive was loved by Jesus.

The amazing thing in this story is not that Jesus healed the leper. The amazing thing is that he reached out to touch the leper. It's a challenge to us to reach out to those who feel left out in our school, our families and our society.

Prayer

Lord – help me to accept the things I can't change.

Lord – give me the courage to change the things I can change.

And, above all, Lord – give me the wisdom to know the difference.

Amen.

The Tempest

Prayer

Just as you calmed the wind

and walked upon the sea,

conquer, my living Lord,

the storms that threaten me.

Amen.

Prayer

Put love in our hearts, Lord Jesus:

love for you,

love for those around us,

love for those we find it hard to like.

Amen.

Prayer

Lord, the kingdom of heaven is a place where there are no more tears, no more pain and no more suffering.

Help us to work towards making this vision a reality here and now.

Amen.

Display Idea for 'Plays of Shakespeare' Theme

Focal point – large picture of the bard himself!

Week 1: *Much Ado About Nothing*

Display adverts for clothes and possessions on one side of the display area. On the other side, display pictures of refugees and/or images of poverty.

Week 2: *The Tempest*

Display extracts of letters to problem pages (things which cause turmoil) from teen magazines.

Week 3: *Romeo and Juliet*

Under the title 'Love One Another', display either a large heart or cross in which pupils can write practical ways they can show love and concern for others.

Week 4: *A Midsummer Night's Dream*

Under the title 'Our Dreams', display either a large thought bubble or a series of smaller thought bubbles in which pupils can write their dreams.

Suggested Songs/Music for 'Plays of Shakespeare' Theme

Week 1: *Much Ado About Nothing*

'No matter what' – Boyzone

'All I once held dear' – Graham Kendrick, from *The Source*

Week 2: *The Tempest*

'Bridge over troubled water' – Simon and Garfunkel

'I will be with you' – Gerard Markland, from *Songs of the Spirit, Liturgical Hymns Old and New*.

'Calm me, Lord' – David Adams and Margaret Rizza, from *Be Still and Know*

'Silent, surrended' – from *The Source*

Week 3: *Romeo and Juliet*

'Love is all around me' – Wet, Wet, Wet

'Love is all you need' – The Beatles

'Flying without wings' – Westlife

Week 4: *A Midsummer Night's Dream*

'Dream' – The Everly Brothers

'Heaven help us all' – Wet, Wet, Wet

Caring for My Neighbour

A four-week series based on Church social teaching

WEEK 1: Option for the Poor

WEEK 2: Equal in Dignity

WEEK 3: All Human Life Is Sacred

WEEK 4: The Common Good

'Prayer of the Week' Posters

Display Ideas

Suggested Songs/Music

WEEK 1 OF 4

Option for the poor

INTRODUCTION

Every day, we make choices – about what we wear; about what we say; about what we eat; about who we are going to spend time with; about what we are going to do. In fact, it could be argued that life is all about making choices – about seeing what options are available and then taking one of them.

This week, we are focusing on the incredibly difficult challenge that followers of Jesus face – the challenge always to take an option for the poor.

We all take this option from time to time – but do we do it often enough? When was the last time you took an option that would benefit the poor? Maybe it was on Comic Relief Day; maybe it was by buying *The Big Issue* in town from one of the homeless; maybe it was by giving some money to the charity collectors outside your local supermarket. Whenever it was – do you think it was enough?

Nobody expects you to change the world, but you can remember the poor as you pray. Maybe, this week, you could pray for the chance to take an option for the poor. Any money you raise won't change the world, but it will make a difference to someone somewhere.

Can your class take an option for the poor?

ACTIVITY

Ask pupils what they are going to have to eat today. Make a list on the board.

Then ask them to work in groups to decide who has been involved in bringing certain items from the field to the table. They could draw a chain – each link being someone involved in the process.

The idea is to remind us that many people are involved in enabling us to eat and for that we should be thankful. Many people today will not eat and we are incredibly lucky to have so much.

Why not say a prayer before you go for dinner this week? This simple grace before meals suffices.

**For what we are about to receive
may the Lord make us truly thankful.**

Amen.

GOSPEL STORY (Matthew 25:31-46)

One of the great parables is about how on Judgement Day we will be separated just as a shepherd separates the sheep and goats. Some will go to heaven – others will hear Jesus say to them:

'I was hungry but you would not feed me, thirsty but you would not give me a drink; I was a stranger but you would not welcome me in your homes, naked but you would not clothe me; I was sick and in prison but you did not take care of me.'

Then they will ask him: 'When, Lord, did we ever see you like this – hungry or thirsty or a stranger or naked or sick or in prison – and did not help you?'

And Jesus will reply, 'I tell you, whenever you refused to help my poor brothers and sisters – you refused to help me.'

These, then, will be sent off to eternal punishment, but the righteous will go to eternal life.

Which group will you be in?
- Do you treat everyone as if they were Jesus?
- Do you take an option for the poor or an option for yourself?
- Do you do something about it – even if only in a very small way?

PRAYER

Brother Jesus – you were born poor;
you fed the hungry;
you loved the outcasts.
Help me to find a way to take an option for the poor.
Amen.

Equal in Dignity

INTRODUCTION

Most supermarkets and producers these days are keen to promote their products as being environmentally friendly and recyclable. But in some countries there are children who are professional recyclers. This sounds rather grand until you consider children like 10-year-old Shireen from India. Shireen scavenges on a city waste tip. If she sells waste paper and plastic bags worth 18p, she will have enough to buy lunch; if not, she goes hungry.

Children like Shireen exist all over the world – in Zaire, they are known as 'sparrows'; in Peru, they are known as 'fruitbirds'. Wherever they are, as they trample through the rubbish heaps, they run the risk of catching all sorts of skin infections and diseases.

When they get older, they often turn to prostitution as it is considered a better alternative.

In Brazil, vigilantes and policemen have murdered tens of thousands of these street kids because they are considered to be a blight on society.

And yet, these are children. They are worthy of love. They deserve to be treated as being equal in dignity. It is only by accident of birth that they live in squalor and we live in comfort.

This week we are challenged to think about how we regard others.
- Do you consider yourself to be superior to others?
- Do you treat others as if you were superior?
- Do you oppress others by what you say to them or by how you look at them?
- How would you treat Shireen – dirty and smelly, uneducated and desperate?

ACTIVITY

The Scripture passage is about everyone being equal in dignity. Ask the class to think of groups of people who are discriminated against – who are not treated as equals. Then construct a charter for equality along the following lines:

We believe that the following are
equal in dignity:
blacks and whites,
Christians and Muslims,
Catholics and Protestants,
rich and poor, etc.

NEW TESTAMENT WRITING (Galatians 3:28)

If you believe in Jesus there can be no difference between Jews and Gentiles, between slaves and free people, between men and women. We are all one in union with Christ Jesus.

This was written by St Paul about 25 years after the death of Jesus. It was part of a letter sent by Paul to a group of Christians living in what we now call Northern Turkey.

It seems that they were having a few problems in accepting that anyone could be a Christian. Paul is quite clear that everyone is to be treated as being *equal in dignity*. What he wrote is amazing if you consider the kind of society Paul lived in. To suggest women should be treated as equals was subversive and revolutionary. Nowadays, we have no problem with equality for the sexes. However, believe it or not, it was only 22 years ago that Britain formally accepted than men and women were equal in dignity. So what Paul wrote was centuries, if not millennia, ahead of its time.

PRAYER

Made in your image – male and female.
Made in your image – black and white.
Made in your image – strong and weak.
Made in your image.
Amen.

WEEK 3 OF 4   All Human Life Is Sacred

INTRODUCTION

Each November, the country looks back and remembers the millions who died in the wars of the last century. This week we reflect on the Church's teaching that all human life is sacred.

The actual word 'sacred' means 'worthy of respect'. So, the Church teaches that all humans are to be respected and treated accordingly. If you asked 100 people if they believed that all human life is sacred you would expect them all to agree, because this idea is such a fundamental aspect of all human societies. People would agree from Paris to Prague; from St Helen's to St Lucia; from Acapulco to Zanzibar. And yet, there are times when we value one person's life above another; there are times when certain groups in society are not deemed to live worthwhile lives; there are times when nations will treat human lives as if they don't matter.

You know that millions died in the two world wars, but did you know that more human lives have been lost because of abortions than in those wars? The most vulnerable form of human life – the unborn foetus – has been massacred. And yet it hardly makes the news. Is that because the victims have no voice to speak out?

In November we keep a minute's silence for those who died. Why not have a minute's silence this week as we think of those who cry a 'silent scream' as they die.

ACTIVITY

Here are some facts about the development of the unborn child in the womb. Simply ask pupils to guess when the different stages of development occur.

When . . .

does the heart start beating?	*25 days*
do the legs and arms begin to form?	*4 weeks*
do bones appear?	*6 weeks*
do fingers and thumbs start forming?	*7 weeks*
do kidneys and other organs form?	*10 weeks*
are the vocal chords formed?	*12 weeks*
does the baby reach half its birth length?	*16 weeks*
do eyebrows and eyelashes start forming?	*20 weeks*

When can abortions be legally carried out?
Up until the twenty-fourth week of pregnancy – when the unborn baby has all the above indicators of being human.

Finish with a simple prayer:

> Thank you, Lord,
> for the precious gift of human life.
> Amen.

OLD TESTAMENT READING (Exodus 20:13)

Do not commit murder.

What a stark reminder to us all. This is one of the Ten Commandments. Notice how it doesn't describe any circumstances in which it is OK to kill.

Over the centuries people seem to have added certain phrases for themselves to make this commandment seem to read:

> Thou shalt not kill unless someone attacks you first – or
> Thou shalt not kill unless the person is a Jew – or
> Thou shalt not kill unless the person is a murderer – and so on.

Some people would argue that it is possible to justify the killing of a fellow human. For example, would it have been justifiable to kill Hitler?

Whichever way you look at it, if this commandment was kept by all, we would have a very different world.

PRAYER

Creator God – the unborn children are yours.
The disabled and infirm are yours.
Everyone in the world is yours.

And Lord, I am yours – help me to make a difference.
Amen.

WEEK 4 OF 4 The Common Good

INTRODUCTION

During November, we remember especially those who lost their lives in armed conflict during the last century. This week, we are going to think about why they were willing to make the sacrifice they did. We can't be sure of the exact reasons but it is not unreasonable to assume that they felt they were defending their country and all the people in it – especially their loved ones. They were willing to take the risk of dying in the cause of the common good – in other words, they did not fight purely for themselves, they fought because the nation as a whole would benefit.

We too can make less dramatic sacrifices in the cause of the common good. Dropping a piece of litter is probably easier for us to do than finding a litter bin, but if we all choose to drop litter, we all suffer. We suffer because we have to trudge through litter and because we have to live in the knowledge that some of our school community do not care about the others in it – the other pupils, staff, cleaners, caretakers, visitors, etc. This is just one example of how small acts of selfishness affect the common good in our school.

However, if we think about how our actions affect others and respond accordingly, each of us can play a part in promoting the common good in our families, school, neighbourhoods, nation and world.

ACTIVITY

Discuss with pupils how one or each of the following affects the development of the common good within their school. A brief example is given.

Graffiti
- affects those who are named – they feel unhappy, their unhappiness is reflected in their attitudes towards others
- affects all who see it – they may think badly of the named person, they may feel they have to laugh about it with others even though they know it's wrong
- affects those who have to clean it up – they may think badly about every individual in the school as they can't be sure who wrote it

- inhibits the development of the common good because relationships are damaged.

Calling people names and gossiping about them

Seeing people being disrespectful towards prefects and doing nothing about it

Lying about why homework has not been done

Telling parents only one side of an incident in school.

NEW TESTAMENT READING
(from **John 6:5-9**)

And Jesus said to them. 'How much food do you have?' Andrew, who was Simon Peter's brother, said, 'There is a boy here who has five loaves of barley bread and two fish. But they will certainly not be enough for all these people.'

This is taken from that famous story of the Feeding of the Five Thousand. No one knows what really happened but this little extract suggests that Andrew – one of the first disciples – has gone to the trouble of finding some food, but stopped once he had found enough for Jesus and the other apostles. Perhaps he was expecting Jesus to send all the people away so they could get on with their own picnic.

After all, what was the point of being apostles if you never got to be with Jesus by yourselves? They were probably fed up with being followed by crowds and having to be glorified 'bouncers' who protected Jesus. Andrew was not thinking of the common good of the 5,000 men and their families who were there. As you know, Jesus took what had been found and transformed it, so that everyone was satisfied. In the same way, Jesus challenges us to see beyond our own needs and seek the common good.

PRAYER

Lord, help us to realise that *all human life is sacred*;

that we are all *equal in dignity*;

that we are called to take an *option for the poor*;

that we should try to act in the cause of the *common good*.

Amen.

Option for the Poor

Brother Jesus – you were born poor;

you fed the hungry;

you loved the outcasts.

Help me to find a way

to take an option for the poor.

Amen.

Equal In Dignity

Made in your image – male and female.

Made in your image – black and white.

Made in your image – strong and weak.

Made in your image.

Amen.

All Human Life Is Sacred

Creator God —
the unborn children are yours.

The disabled and infirm are yours.

Everyone in the world is yours.

And Lord, I am yours —
help me to make a difference.

Amen.

The Common Good

Lord, help us to realise

that **all human life is sacred**;

that we are all **equal in dignity**;

that we are called

to take an **option for the poor**;

that we should try to act

in the cause of the **common good**.

Amen.

Display Idea for 'Caring for My Neighbour' Theme

Set aside some wall space for these four weeks and build up
a display around the focal point of a globe.

Week 1: Option for the Poor

Selection of Tear Fund, Christian Aid and Oxfam posters, perhaps with a selection of
'Traidcraft' goods.

Week 2: Equal in Dignity

Collage of newspaper/magazine cuttings illustrating inequality in the world.

Week 3: All Human Life Is Sacred

Display information from this week's activity, perhaps with information about
the Samaritans.

Week 4: The Common Good

Newspaper cuttings and magazine extracts about environmental issues.

Relevant Songs/Music for 'Caring for My Neighbour' Theme

Week 1: Option for the Poor
'Feed the world' – Band Aid
'Dancing with the missing' – Sting
'Another day for you and me in Paradise' – Phil Collins

Week 2: Equal in Dignity
'He ain't heavy – he's my brother' – The Hollies
'As long as you love me' – Backstreet Boys
'One love' – Bob Marley

Week 3: All Human Life Is Sacred
'Papa don't preach' – Madonna
'Wonder Child' – Mary Black

Week 4: The Common Good
'World in union' – The Rugby Union World Cup Theme
'A brand new start' – Paul Weller
'Larger than life' – Backstreet Boys
'One' – U2

A three-week series based on

The X-Files
The Truth Is in You!

Week 1: Yeti and Nessie??

Week 2: Flying Saucers??

Week 3: The *Marie Celeste*??

'Prayer of the Week' Posters

Display Ideas

Suggested Songs/Music

Week 1 of 3

The X-Files – The Truth Is in You!

Yeti and Nessie?

Theme

One of the most popular TV programmes in recent years has been *The X-Files*. As we approached the end of the second millennium since the birth of Jesus, it seemed we were fascinated by things we couldn't really explain or prove – and still can't! Over the next few weeks we're going to look at some of these and ask: 'Is the truth out there in the world, or is truth something you experience for yourself on the inside?'

There have long been sightings of ape-like creatures. In the Himalayan mountain range the creature is referred to as the Abominable Snowman or the Yeti. It has been sighted by, among others, Sherpa Tensing Norgay, who accompanied Sir Edmund Hillary in the first conquest of Mount Everest. There have been many expeditions to try to find the Yeti, but all have failed to provide the conclusive evidence sceptics require. But what about you? How much proof do you need before you believe something? This week maybe you'll find out!

Would you believe it?

In 1938, off the coast of South Africa, a group of fishermen caught a fish of a type they'd never seen before. Eventually, some scientists found out that the fish was a species called the 'coelacanth', never before seen by humans. The coelacanth is dark brown in colour and grows to more than five feet in length, weighing more than ten stone. Unlike most fish, it gives birth to live young as opposed to laying eggs.

What was truly remarkable was that this species was thought to be extinct and could only be identified thanks to fossils dated as more than 300 million years old! So, a species which lived at the time of the dinosaurs is still alive today!

Would you have believed it?

Daily Prayer

Lord, it is so difficult to believe sometimes.
Help me to keep searching for the truth.
When I am ready, help me to make the leap of faith
that leads to knowing you.
Amen.

Activity

Which of the following is easy to prove?

- Dinosaurs existed.

- The Loch Ness Monster exists.

- You love someone.

- There is a place called America.

- There is a place called Heaven.

- Humans are evolved from apes.

- The earth is in orbit round the sun.

- A man called Jesus lived about 2,000 years ago
  in an area which is now called Israel.

- The universe was created by a big explosion.

- There was something there before the universe existed.

- God made the world in seven days.

- God is important to some people when things go wrong.

Each of these points could prove a good starter for discussion.

Week 2 of 3

The X-Files – The Truth Is in You!

Flying Saucers?

Theme

For thousands of years, people have looked up at the stars and wondered at their beauty, but it is only relatively recently that we have become preoccupied with the question, 'Are we alone or is there life elsewhere in the universe?'

The phenomenon of Unidentified Flying Objects or flying saucers has been a common theme explored in twentieth century culture. The film *Close Encounters of the Third Kind* tells the story of one man's obsession with this idea. If you've seen *ET*, you'll know it concerns an encounter with extraterrestrials. The idea of alien abduction is often referred to in the programme *The X-Files*.

- So, are we alone?

- Will you have to see an alien to believe they exist?

- Will you have to see God before you believe?

Would you believe it?

- Between 1947 and 1969, the United States Air Force investigated 12,000 UFO sightings of which 701 remain unexplained!

- H. G. Wells wrote *The War of the Worlds* – a book about an alien invasion – in 1898, nearly a century before the film *Independence Day* was made!

- The cult of the UFO is such that in one Wigan paper there is a weekly column which records sightings over Wigan!

Would you believe it?

Daily prayer

Lord, it is so difficult to believe sometimes.
Help me to realise that you are always with me.
Amen.

Activity

The following is best delivered as a meditation, where pupils close their eyes and try to imagine the scene as it develops. Some gentle instrumental music in the background helps to set the right mood. Read through quite slowly, giving participants a chance to think.

Imagine you are in your room alone, late at night. You hear a sound outside and go out of the front door to investigate. You hear a whirring sound coming from above. You look up and see a flying saucer. It seems to be descending. The whirring sound gets louder and, as it draws nearer, you become aware of coloured lights on its underside. Gently it descends and lands just a few yards away from you. The whirring sound stops.

A door opens and a radiant light shines out, making you shield your eyes. After a few seconds your eyes adjust and you are able to look into the light. Out steps a being. What does it look like? It approaches you and you feel at ease with it. You feel drawn towards it and soon you are standing opposite each other. You don't feel threatened. The creature greets you, saying it comes in peace. What does its voice sound like?

It says it can help you to achieve anything, as long as it is good not just for you, but for others too. It says it could help you to end hunger in the world; to bring healing to people; to make everyone equal. You think carefully. What do you ask for? The creature tells you that you can make a difference; that you can achieve your goal, but that you have to start small, with your friends and family, and that sometimes you may feel like you are achieving nothing. The creature says that if you talk to it in your mind when you feel down, you will be heard. It leaves with the words: 'I will be with you – even when you can't see me – I will be with you.' And in a sudden blinding flash of light the creature is gone and you are alone.

You go back to your room and know that life will never be the same again.

Week 3 of 3

The X-Files – The Truth Is in You!

The Marie Celeste?

Theme

On 5 November 1872, the American brig, the *Marie Celeste*, set sail from New York. A month and a day later it was spotted by the crew of the *Dei Gratia* sailing erratically in the Atlantic between the Azores and Portugal.

The *Dei Gratia* came alongside it and the crew boarded the *Marie Celeste*. The ship was deserted. The ship's log had last been filled in on 25 November, suggesting it had sailed without crew for nine days and had managed to travel 700 miles north-east in that time.

The crew's quarters were undamaged and the crew's belongings were all apparently there. The cargo was intact apart from a keg of alcohol, which appeared damaged. There was no evidence of a struggle but the ship's lifeboat was no longer on the ship.

What could have happened?

Would you believe it?

- The captain of the *Marie Celeste* had dinner the day before departure with the captain of the *Dei Gratia* – the very ship which found the *Marie Celeste* deserted in the vast expanse of the Atlantic Ocean.

- The *Marie Celeste* had originally been called the *Amazon* and its first captain had died within 48 hours of its launch.

- *Dei Gratia* means 'Thank God'.

Would you believe it?

Daily prayer

Lord, we never know what is going to happen in our lives.
Help us to live each moment knowing you are here with us.
Amen.

Activity

The story of the *Marie Celeste* has enthralled enthusiasts of the unexplained for over a century. All sorts of theories have been put forward to explain it. Here are some of those theories:

- the ship was attacked by a giant octopus-like creature called the Kraken

- the crew all got drunk and fell overboard

- the crew were abducted by aliens

- the ship was overcome by a freak storm and the crew was thrown overboard.

It would certainly make a great film. Your activity this week is to write a synopsis (summary of a story-line) to present to a Hollywood producer.

Those on board the ship were Captain Briggs, his wife and daughter and a crew of seven men. You can decide who you want to star in it and what characters they might play.

Yeti and Nessie??

Would you believe it?

~ In 1938, off the coast of South Africa, a group of fishermen caught a fish of a type they'd never seen before. Eventually, some scientists found out that the fish was a species called the 'coelacanth', never before seen by humans.

~ The coelacanth is dark brown in colour and grows to more than five feet in length, weighing more than ten stone. Unlike most fish, it gives birth to live young as opposed to laying eggs.

~ What was truly remarkable was that this species was thought to be extinct and could only be identified thanks to fossils dated as more than 300 million years old! So, a species which lived at the time of the dinosaurs is still alive today!

Would you have believed it?

THE TRUTH

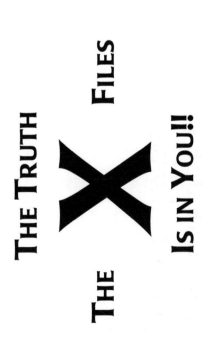

FILES

THE   IS IN YOU!!

Daily Prayer

Lord, it is so difficult to believe sometimes.

Help me to keep searching for the truth.

When I am ready, help me to make the leap of faith that leads to knowing you.

Amen.

Flying Saucers??

Would you believe it?

 Between 1947 and 1969, the United States Air Force investigated 12,000 UFO sightings of which 701 remain unexplained!

 H. G. Wells wrote *The War of the Worlds* – a book about an alien invasion – in 1898, nearly a century before the film *Independence Day* was made!

 The cult of the UFO is such that in one Wigan paper there is a weekly column which records sightings over Wigan!

Would you believe it?

THE TRUTH

X

FILES

THE IS IN YOU!!

Daily Prayer

Lord, it is so difficult to believe sometimes.

Help me to realise that you are always with me.

Amen.

The Marie Celeste ??

Would you believe it?

 The captain of the *Marie Celeste* had dinner the day before departure with the captain of the *Dei Gratia* – the very ship which found the *Marie Celeste* deserted in the vast expanse of the Atlantic Ocean.

 The *Marie Celeste* had originally been called the *Amazon* and its first captain had died within 48 hours of its launch.

 Dei Gratia means 'Thank God'.

Would you believe it?

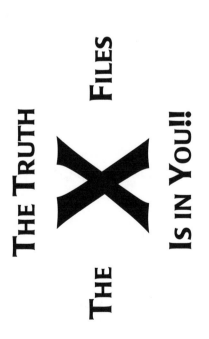
Daily Prayer

Lord, we never know what is going to happen in our lives.

Help us to live each moment knowing you are here with us.

Amen.

DISPLAY IDEA FOR 'THE X-FILES' THEME

Wall display: silver lettering mounted on black; dark-blue backing paper. Selection of *X-Files* posters and/or video cases.

The X-FILES

The Truth Is in You!

Week 1: Yeti and Nessie

Create a large footprint in 'snow': Make a template of a footprint and place it on a polystyrene tile or heavy-duty white card. Then spray glue around it and sprinkle polystyrene beads on glue. After a few sprayings and layers of beads this looks quite convincing.

Week 2: Flying Saucers

Make a flying saucer from cardboard. Cover it with aluminium foil or shiny paper and dangle it from the ceiling.

Week 3: The *Marie Celeste*

Place a table laid with a few pieces of crockery next to the wall. On the wall just above the table stick two triangular pieces of cloth to represent the sails of a ship.

SUGGESTED SONGS/MUSIC FOR 'THE X-FILES' THEME

Week 1: Yeti and Nessie

'The monster mash' – The Beach Boys
Jurassic Park theme – John Williams

Week 2: Flying Saucers

'You are not alone' – Michael Jackson
Close Encounters of the Third Kind theme – John Williams
ET theme – John Williams

Week 3: The *Marie Celeste*

'Sailing' – Rod Stewart